EDGAR

Paintings

LEOPARD

This edition published in 1995 by Leopard Books
Random House, 20 Vauxhall Bridge Road, London SW1V 2SA

ISBN 0 7529 0037 4
Printed and bound in Portugal by
Printer Portuguesa Lda

"One must have a high opinion of a work of art—not the work one is creating at the moment, but of that which one desires to achieve one day. Without this it is not worthwhile working." [1]

—EDGAR DEGAS

1. *Duke and Duchess of Morbilli* c. 1865

2. *The Bellelli Family* c. 1858-60

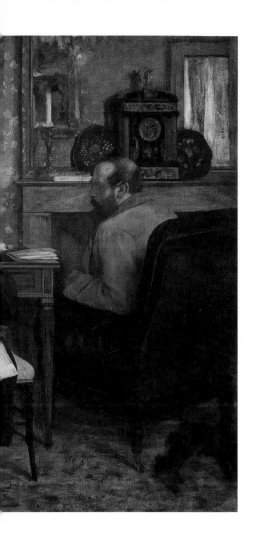

3. *Portrait of Hortonse Valpincon*

4. *Madame René de Gas* 1872-73

5. *Before the Ballet* 1888

6. *The Dance Class* c. 1874

7. *The Rehearsal of the Ballet on Stage* c. 1874

8. *Dancers Rocking Back and Forth* 1879

9. *Miss LaLa at the Cirque Fernando* 1879

10. *Café Concert Aux Ambassadeurs* c. 1876

11. *At the Café Concert: "The Song of the Dog"* 1875-77

12. *The Orchestra*

13. *Dance Foyer at the Opera in the rue Le Peletier* 1872

14. *Muscians of the Orchestra*   c. 1870

15. *Women on a Café Terrace, Evening* 1877

16. *A Frieze of Dancers*

17. *Young Dancer and Woman with Umbrella on a Bench*

18. *At the Café (L'Absinthe)* 1875-76

19. *Laundresses* c. 1884-86

20. *Woman Ironing* 1882

21. *Woman in a Tub*

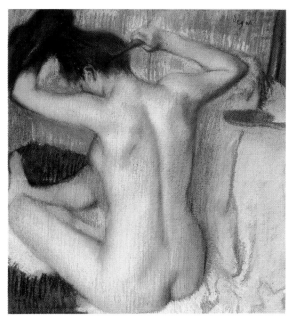

22. *Woman Combing her Hair* c. 1885

23. *Carriage at the Races* 1869

24. *Jockeys in Front of the Grandstands* c. 1866-68

25. *Jockeys Before the Start of the Race* c. 1878-80

26. *The Milliner's Shop* 1882

27. *The Ballerina*

28. *Blue Dancers* 1890

29. *Two Ballerinas* 1874

Afterword

Born in Paris in 1834, Edgar Degas was obsessed with becoming an artist even as a child. Although, as was expected of a proper bourgeois gentleman, Degas entered law school in 1853, two years later he began studying art with a disciple of Ingres. While other young artists of the period denigrated Ingres as a reactionary, his mastery of line and contour captivated Degas and throughout his career Degas followed Ingres's stress on the importance of draftsmanship in art. The works of Mantegna, Uccello, and other masters of the fifteenth century that he discovered on trips to Italy in 1856, 1858 and 1859 also profoundly affected Degas's vision and goals as an artist.

Between 1860 and 1865, Degas's work reflected his preoccupation with traditional iconography—historical, religious, and mythological themes dominated his paintings; his *The Suffering of the Town of Orleans*, done in the classical manner and accepted by the official Salon of Paris in 1865, won him much critical praise. It is, however, in Degas's portrait work of this period—*Duke and Duchess of Morbilli* (plate 1), *Portrait of Hortonse Valpincon* (plate 3) and *Self-Portrait* (title page)—that the synthesis of what Degas learned from the masters and his own individual creativity was fully realized. One of his early masterpieces, *The Bellelli Family* (plate 2), is tightly structured in the manner of classical portraiture. It is unlikely, however, that it would have been accepted by the official

Salon had Degas chosen to submit it: although one daughter looks out at the viewer in the "accepted" manner of nineteenth-century portraiture, and the Baroness maintains a rigid, "classical" demeanor, the casual pose of the younger daughter and the depiction of the Baron, distracted momentarily from his work, fly in the face of the standards favored by the Academy. In *Musicians of the Orchestra* (plate 14), executed in 1870, Degas's innovative approach to group portraiture—particularly his experiments with unusual viewpoints and asymmetry—is even more striking.

In mid-nineteenth-century Paris, traditional assumptions and prescriptions were being questioned in every art. Zola, Duranty, Edmond de Goncourt, and other writers were revolutionizing French literature with their realistic descriptions of the contemporary scene; the poet Baudelaire exhorted artists to become men of the world, to focus on the world around them and record it for posterity. Realism gradually made its way into Degas's portraits: "One must," Degas wrote, "paint portraits of people in typical and familiar attitudes and, above all, give to their faces the same expression as one gives to their bodies."[2]

In his movement away from idealized images to more natural, informal representations, Degas is closely associated with the Impressionist movement. Like Renoir, Monet, and the other Independents, Degas was also fierce in his opposition to the art establishment—as embodied by the official Salon of Paris—and its inflexible adherence to the standards of academic art. But while Degas contributed works to seven of the eight Impressionist exhibitions, his intentions and his achievements differed from those of the Impressionists in important ways, and he objected to being identified with them. Both his technique and subject matter set Degas apart. The Impressionists sought to capture the play of light and atmosphere as it is perceived by the artist's eye, an effect they achieved in the patches of color and blurred contours characteristic of their pastoral landscape paintings. Degas insisted that line and contour were the basis of art; moreover, his interest lay not in the pastoral but in urban settings—the theater, the ballet, the race-course. The Impressionists were concerned with the movement of light and shadow, Degas in the movement of the human body. And while Degas's paintings, like theirs, present a moment caught in time, Degas carefully constructed his compositions to achieve this "casual" look.

Carriage at the Races (plate 23) and *Jockeys in Front of the Grandstands* (plate 24), early examples of Degas's race-course pictures, have, in their strong design and clear colors, an almost documentary vividness and reality.[3] From the highly trained horses of the race track, exquisite in their movement, Degas turned his attentions to a subject that is perhaps the epitome of precise and beautiful movement—the ballet dancer. Not content only to show dancers as the audience sees them, Degas literally went behind the scenes. In his paintings of dancers in rehearsal or in class, Degas penetrates the dancer's world, capturing the intensity of their rituals, their exacting and demanding exercises, and even their attitudes toward their occupation. These pictures are alive with the tensions of the moment; in *Dance Foyer at the Opera in the rue Le Peletier* (plate 13), for example, the emptiness of the room adds to the stark atmosphere Degas sought to create. Degas spent many hours observing dancers, his eye constantly alert to new perceptions: "One has to repeat the same thing ten or rather a hundred times," he wrote. "In art nothing must be left to accident—not even movement."[4] His continual discoveries of different aspects of the "same" scene is apparent: the inattentive, even graceless, dancers in The *Dance Class* (plate 6) present an image much less flattering than the one offered in *The Rehearsal of the Ballet on Stage* (plate 7) and other earlier works. His paintings evolved from all-encompassing views of dancers on stage or in a rehearsal hall to close-up views of individual dancers or groups of dancers. In works like *Two Ballerinas* (plate 29), *Dancers Rocking Back and Forth* (plate 8) and *A Frieze of Dancers* (plate 16), Degas removed the dancers from their "background" both literally and figuratively; no longer does one see the hard work of learning the craft; swirls of color become the essence of dance and of movement.

Popular diversions and daily life in the city provided another source of inspiration for Degas. *Café Concert Aux Ambassadeurs* (plate 10) and *At the Café Concert: "The Song of the Dog"* (plate 11) vibrate with the atmosphere of nineteenth-century Paris, where social classes mixed at concerts and cafes, indulging in risque or flirtatious encounters. As in his ballet studies, Degas mixed dark tones with brilliant flashes of color to achieve eye-catching contrasts and textures.

Degas was intrigued, too, by Parisian low-life. Like the naturalist novelist Zola, whose novels dealt objectively with the underclass, Degas probed into the dark and often desperate lives of prostitutes. Both *At the Café (L'Absinthe)* (plate 18) and *Women on a Café Terrace, Evening* (plate 15) are morally neutral works; Degas's use of drab colors conveys only a mood of alienation and loneliness, while the unusual perspective and unexpected angles endow these paintings with a sense of real-life immediacy. This latter quality reflects the impact of the new art of photography on Degas's work, an influence visible, too, in *Jockeys Before the Start of the Race* (plate 25) which breaks every traditional rule of composition and, as Patrick Bade notes, could be "a kind of snapshot carelessly taken with a Kodak camera."[5]

Degas's famous studies of women in their private spheres, a motif that would occupy him from the mid-1880s to the end of his life, mark not only a highpoint of Degas's career, but a radical new approach to the female nude, a subject that had dominated Western art since the Renaissance. Degas reportedly declared, "Hitherto the nude has always been represented in poses which presuppose an audience, but these women of mine are honest, simple folk, unconcerned by any other interest than those involved with their physical conditions."[6] In such paintings as *Woman in a Tub* (plate 21) and *Woman Combing Her Hair* (plate 22), the women Degas portrayed indeed seem to be caught unawares in intimate moments. While many people, including the critic Huysman,[7] considered these works insulting to women, for Degas, these representations are, like his other works, primarily meant to disclose the infinite variety of movements of the human body. Degas's rejection of a romantic, idealized concept of women reached its extreme expression in his series of paintings dealing with women involved in mundane, fatiguing occupations like *Woman Ironing* (plate 20) and *Laundresses* (plate 19).

Degas was one of the great independent spirits of the nineteenth century: throughout his life he maintained a disdain for the art establishment and refused all official honors and awards. An artist and innovator of rare ability, he mastered the classical style of Ingres, understood and assimilated Delacroix's lessons on the use of color, and brought an unprecedented realism to each of his works of art. Despite his protestations, he was a seminal figure in the Impressionist movement, influencing Renoir, Monet, Cassatt, and many others; unlike many of his generation, he appreciated works of more "modern" artists like Van Gogh, Cézanne, Gauguin, and Toulouse-Lautrec, amassing an impressive collection of their works in the years before his death in 1917.

Known for his witty, often harsh, judgements of other artists, Degas was held in high esteem by all his contemporaries, even those who, like Renoir and Pissarro, were the objects of his criticism. His friend Edmond de Goncourt wrote, "So far of all the men I have seen, he has been the one who has best caught the atmosphere of modern life and the spirit of the present." [8] But perhaps Paul Valéry provides the best description of this iconoclastic genius. He was, Valéry declared, "the epitome of the pure artist...driven by an acute preoccupation with truth."[9]

NOTES

1. Eduard Huttinger, *Degas* (New York: Crown Publishers), 8
2. Ibid, 41
3. Ibid, 49
4. Ibid, 67
5. Patrick Bade, *Degas: the Masterworks* (New York: Portland House), 108
6. Rachel Barnes, Editor, *Degas by Degas* (New York: Alfred A. Knopf), 62
7. Huttinger, 80
8. Ibid, 41
9. Paul Valéry, *Degas, Manet, Morisot* (New York: Pantheon Books), xxxiii

List of Plates

The photographs in this book were supplied by: